Sociocracy For All is a nonprofit operating globally and registered in
Massachusetts, USA. www.sociocracyforall.org
All content is licensed under a CC-SA-BY-NC license. 2023
ISBN 978-1-949183-23-8

Table of contents

Preparing a meeting 1

Holding a meeting 12
   Meeting format 13
   Time management 25
   Rounds 32

Processes 35
   Making decisions 36
   Selection process 42
   Defining roles 44
   Drafting a proposal 46
   Performance reviews 48

Common Questions 53

Templates and checklists 60

Learning more 61

Who prepares the agenda?

A prepared meeting is often a better meeting! Groups differ on who prepares it. In some groups, it's the leader, facilitator, and secretary who prepare a draft agenda. But it's also ok for one or two people to prepare the agenda, for example, the leader or the leader and the facilitator.

Just be clear and make an agreement so it's clear who is on meeting prep.

Why prepare an agenda?

It's possible to "wing" it and work with an instant agenda. But some preparation can speed up and provide clarity for the meeting.

- Having clarity on what's needed as a next step can make agenda items faster because it's clear to what ends we're talking about a topic.
- Some preparatory work like preparing proposals or gathering information for input can save meeting time.

Additional prep work might be part of identified roles, like sending a meeting reminder, sharing relevant documents or the agenda beforehand, or reserving a room.

What are meetings for?

Meetings create clarity for our work.

Reports are for sharing information.

One or more people have information to share about a topic that the rest of the group needs to hear. For example, they have completed a piece of work, or researched new information.

To make sure that the information has been received, be sure to leave time for questions.

 You're done with the agenda item when the information has been passed on successfully.

Explorations are for brainstorming, feedback or reactions.

Someone brings a topic and explains it, and then the group responds with their ideas.

Examples:
- Someone has an idea and wants to hear the other group members' reactions.
- A role identifies an issue and needs ideas how to solve it.
- Based on a need identified by the group, a group brainstorms proposal ideas.
- Something happened and the group wants to exchange ideas.

 It's complete when enough ideas have been shared.

We make **decisions** when an action or policy needs to be chosen.

Either a proposal is already prepared and we use the consent process (see page 37), or we draft a proposal and decide then.

 It's complete when there is consent.

Reporting (with questions)

Give a prompt, **receive** input, feedback or ideas

Decisions include
- hearing the proposal & answering questions
- a reaction round
- the consent decision.

What's an easy way to prepare an agenda?

Start with a template! It frames the steps that are always the same and ensure good quality, inclusion and flow in the meeting.

Every meeting has the opening and and closing. The agenda items are in between like a sandwich.

You can see a full template on page 62.

Meeting agenda

Opening (Check-in and ADMIN)

Agenda items
_____
_____
_____
_____

Closing

What should we talk about?

Ideally, you have a repository of open topics; we call that the backlog or "parking lot".

It's a simple list of topics to talk about in the future.

From the backlog, pick the most pressing or important topics and sort them into an order that makes sense.

No backlog?

It might make sense to start a backlog.

Until you have one, look at last time's notes. Where did you leave off?

Ask your circle members for their needs. What do they need to talk about so work can continue productively?

Sequencing complex decisions

Decisions often take longer than one meeting. In that case, package it into three steps:
- understanding the issue
- exploring solutions and drafting a proposal
- approving a proposal and implementing it

meeting 1	meeting 2	meeting 3
understand the issue	explore solutions	approve proposal

Super prepared agendas

You can try and see if it helps you and your group to prepare an agenda like this:

What are we trying to do?

Pick report, exploration or decision so you are on the same on what you want to accomplish.

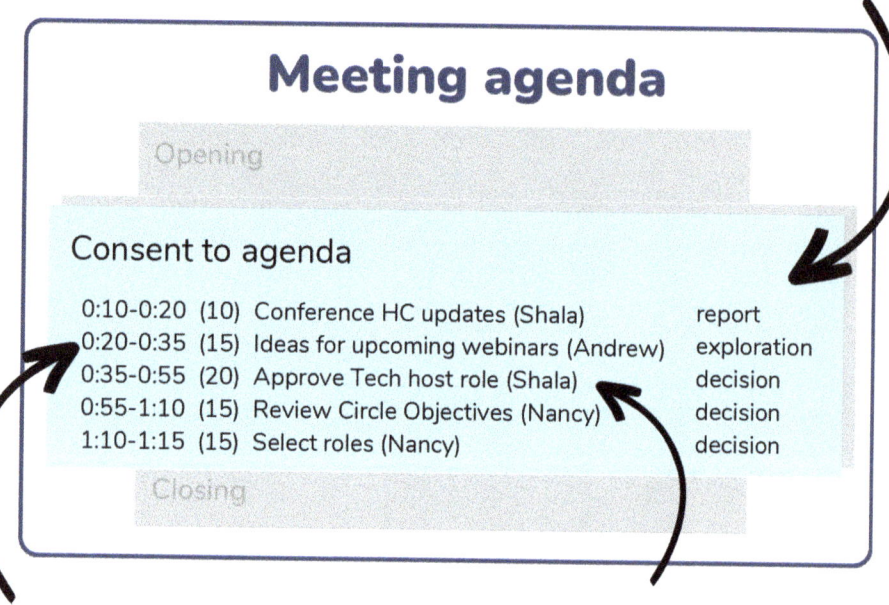

Time your agenda

It helps to plan the beginning and end time for for an item - that way, we see at a glance whether we're on track!

Who is holding the item?

Who is prepared to provide context? Who has requested for the circle to talk about this item?

How much time to plan?

Of course, it depends on culture, complexity and style but I plan like this:
- a report takes 5-10 min
- an exploration takes 15-25 min
- a decision takes 10-20 if the proposal is prepared and 20-40 min if we start from scratch

A healthy mix

A good meeting "mix" is
- under 20% meeting time on reports
- at least 25% of meeting time on explorations. That way, we can make good use of the shared expertise in the room.
- Move at least one item to a decision per meeting to get completion.

Holding a meeting

Meeting format

We follow a very simple meeting format

- **Opening**: Making sure people & circle are ready for the meeting
- **Content**: Creating more clarity for the circle's work.
- **Closing**: Evaluating the meeting to improve meetings over time.

We will now go through each of the phases separately.

> Opening Round/check-in
> ADMIN
>
> Consent to agenda
> Agenda Items
> Update Backlog
>
> Closing Round

Opening round (check-in)

We start the meeting as human beings.
Everyone comes in with a story, a context, an immediate experience previous to the meeting.

This might be rush hour in the metro, a spilled coffee, a newborn baby, a divorce, a death in the family, frustration with another circle, gratitude about spring weather, experiencing pride towards accomplished work and tasks, anxiety about an agenda item in the upcoming meeting or just the desire for a third cup of coffee.

Check-ins - even if it's just a handful of minutes, are known to increase psychological safety in a group. Psychological safety is a big success factor in effective groups so check-ins are worth the time!

When we have shared whatever affects us in the moment, we are ready to shift our attention to the circle business.

Keep check-ins to about one minute each person, or less.

ADMIN

The human beings in the room might be ready for the meeting now but the circle still needs to get ready in the ADMIN phase.

Attendance: We make sure our note taker is present, and we take note of who is absent. This creates a caring culture and helps build a good agenda.

Duration: How long will this meeting take? Who has to leave early or very much on time?

Minutes: Have last meeting's minutes been consented to and have they been published in the logbook? Have people who missed last time's minutes read and understood the minutes? In short: are we all on the same page and up to date?

Information: Is there anything else people want to share? Like an organizational announcement, an invitation or a travel notice?

Next meeting: Is there a next meeting date? If not, is there a plan on when and how the circle is coming to the next meeting date?

Any of these things can be put on the agenda if they are complicated.

For example scheduling a meeting time, or dealing with someone's absence, or an objection about last time's decision from someone who missed the meeting.

In the ADMIN phase, it's about moving things along quick. The actual meeting time will be negotiated next so move it along!

Consenting to the agenda

We plan an agenda, but before we actually start, we need the circle's consent to the agenda - quick thumbs up from everyone is enough.

> Does this agenda look good enough?

Meeting time is precious time - setting our topics together, so they work for everyone is an important part of collaboration!

By adjusting and consenting to the agenda, the circle takes responsibility for the agenda. This includes the order of topics, the timing (more or less), and the desired outcomes (report, exploration, decision).

We **all** make an effort to stay true to our commitment, and it does not solely lie on the facilitator to make the meeting successful.

> Don't consent to an agenda that you don't understand!

If there is an objection, we try to find a solution that works for everyone in the circle.

A few examples:

"The agenda doesn't include xyz, and it's an urgent topic."

"I propose to swap that topic in and postpone topic 5 instead."

"We're not prepared enough to talk about agenda item xyz because not everyone read the document."

"I propose we include a 5 min reading time."

"This agenda is too long."

"Maybe we could delegate item 4 to a subgroup and focus on the rest today?"

Agenda items

Now it's time to talk about our agenda items.
Give reports, explore and make decisions.

- For reports, let the person report and make sure people can ask questions so the information is received.
- For explorations, let someone give the prompt and then do rounds until all relevant ideas or reactions have been shared.
- For decisions, use the consent process (p. 17).

Adjusting the agenda

It's quite possible that the agenda doesn't work as planned and consented. Something might take longer or be more complicated than you anticipated.

If you notice you've gone astray more than you want, make sure to update the agenda and get consent.

- speed up
- postpone agenda items
- extend the meeting
- ...

Remember your desired outcomes!

Remember reports, explorations and decisions?
It's easy to lose time by discussing things that we don't need to discuss. Be clear in your expectations and prompts.

Groups easily lose time by discussing a report - although a simple share of information was enough.

It's also easy to get into endless discussions when a simple proposal would have gotten consent. Sometimes groups seem to wait for a magic solution to fall from the sky - but it's ok to shortcut a discussion by picking an idea, propose it and adopt it if there are no objections.

"Are there any topics we should talk about next time?"

Backlog review

Once we've talked about all items and we've completed our content of the meeting, it's a good practice to ask if there are **new topics** that have come up during the meeting that should be addressed in future meetings.

For example, if the meeting surfaces a bigger issue, make sure to write it down on your backlog.

Asking for new items doesn't take long, about 1-3 minutes.

The backlog is filled during but also between meetings with all topics that we need to talk about to do our work.

Review dates for policies or roles can also be listed on the backlog so they don't get forgotten on future agenda items.

From time to time, a circle might do a longer backlog review where all backlog items are looked at to get on the same page on prioritization and to see if items are still current - like spring cleaning!

Closing round

We close the meeting with a meeting evaluation where each member, in a round, highlights their observations and reflections on the meeting. The goal is to improve meetings over time, and make them work for our group.

During that check-out, circle members can reflect on anything that seems relevant to them. Typically, you can give useful feedback on:

- interpersonal dynamics (gratitude, tension, style of communication, sense of connection etc.)
- the content of the work (how much got done, how much clarity was created, was a difficult topic finally dealt with etc.) and
- the process of the meeting (did the facilitation feel firm enough/too rigid, was the meeting time kept, did the choice of agenda items seem relevant, was there crosstalk during rounds etc.)

Bored with your closing rounds? Try out our card decks of check-out prompts!

They include feedback on
- **process**
- **content**
- **interpersonal**

www.sociocracyforall.org/cards

Time management

stay on topic

How most groups lose time

- Agenda not prepared clear enough and it takes to long for the circle to understand what they are asked to do.

- People who stray off topic aren't reminded.

- Staying in reactions after reactions when a proposal could be made.

- Lots of one-off (operational) decisions when policies could be made to answer several issues.

- Not enough leadership in moving operations along; tasks should not take a lot of meeting time but instead be followed up upon between meetings.

- Not enough leadership in moving operations along; tasks should not take a lot of meeting time but instead be followed up upon between meetings.

- Too many long reports. (Try to type them and read them instead of doing them out loud.)

- Agenda items aren't what actually needs to be talked about but just busy work. (Not everything that is being done in the circle also needs to be talked about each meeting!)

- Too much time on preferences, too little time on circle-critical discussions.

- Not enough clarity about the processes (not enough training)

get organized
get trained
hold each other accountable

Typical traps

Groups can work together effectively if there is only one topic at the same time. Facilitators need to help figure out what topic is the current one. Multi-tasking is impossible as a group!
These are some typical patterns and how to maneuver out of them.

Topic drifts
- ⚠ the circle goes off topic
- ✓ remind people of the topic

Fork
- ⚠ the circle needs to decide between two topics
- ✓ help make a decision between both topics

Dependency
- ⚠ the circle needs to solve one issue before solving the current one
- ✓ be clear: let's solve this first and then come back

Tracking time

A typical way to lose time is for people to go off topic - steer them back. Ideally, you acknowledge and validate the topic they care about and also remind them of the current topic.

A gentle way of doing that is by offering to make time for the discussion - but not without being intentional about it!

bla off topic bla bla
bla bla off topic bla
bla bla bla bla bla bla
bla off topic bla bla
off topic bla bla

I can see that this is very important to you.
Do you want to make room in the agenda for it now and see what we can postpone, or shall we put it on the backlog?

"Looks like we're going over time and I want to make sure we can complete this topic. I propose we add 15min here and ... postpone the last item/extend the meeting, etc."

Changing the agenda

You can change the agenda based on needs that come up in the meeting. It just requires consent again.
Just make a quick proposal and ask for objections. Then continue with the new plan. (Of course if there are objections, the group needs to figure out a different proposal.)

This is not only important for staying in integrity and being intentional with our but also to make sure that the new agenda still works for everyone.

Rounds

Rounds are a useful way to stay on track and hear everyone's voice.

It's very simple: whenever we want to hear what circle members have to say, we call a round and speak one by one.

Facilitators can put themselves into the middle of the round so they can speak as members of the circle. Or simply state "as a circle member, I think...", or "putting my facilitator hat on, let's move to the next topic."

What kinds of rounds are there?

Questions rounds — Used to make sure every circle member can get their questions answered.
Answer directly or gather all questions and then answer all at once.

Reaction rounds — Used to gather ideas or reactions. You can do more than one round. People can also pass if they have nothing to add.

Consent rounds — Used to see if each circle member consents to a proposal. (If someone objects, complete the round before addressing the objection!)

Calling rounds

In an in-person meeting, it can be simple because the seating arrangement might make it clear what the order is.
Start somewhere and ask people to take their turns.
Then the person next to them speaks.

In virtual meetings, you can have the facilitator call out 2 names, like "Amy is going to speak and then Shala." (And then later: "now Shala and then Andrew")
Some facilitators also put the names of the circle members into the chat and create a "seating order" that way, or you find a tool that provides a randomized order.

Rounds and pace

Rounds shouldn't feel stifled or slow. Rounds are most productive when the prompt is clear, and talking turns are on the short side. It also helps when people pass when they don't have anything new to say. Model that and behavior will change over time.

Short cuts

It's ok to take short cuts from time to time. Examples:

- Instead of asking for verbal consent, go for thumbs up.
- Instead of doing a questions round, ask for raised hands in case of questions.

Short cuts are useful but the are also risky - it's much more likely to lose nuances or prevent someone from speaking up if we take shortcuts. Aim for a good mix of "full" processes and shortcuts where it makes sense.

Processes

Making decisions

Understanding an issue

When a new issue comes to the circle, it's good to understand what it's about. That can be quick - or it can be a deeper process.

Only rush to solutions before the issue when it's sufficiently understood - do rounds until you feel clear about it.

Exploring options + drafting a proposal

What could be done about the issue? What options do we have?

Draft a proposal. You can draft it together imply by gathering ideas in rounds.

For complex issues, you can try gathering dimensions first.
(See process "drafting a proposal" on page 47.)

Make a decision (consent process)

Clarifying questions	Give everyone a chance to ask questions. about the proposal.
Quick reactions	Let everyone say how they feel and what they think about the proposal.
Consent round	Ask if people consent or object.

Everyone in the circle needs to consent for the proposal to pass.

Consent and objections

Consent does not mean that everyone needs to **agree**.

For a consent decision, it's enough when no one has an objection. That way, it's easier to make decisions and move forward with something we can try.

Facilitators might need to remind people not to get too attached to their preferences - we can work together more easily if we find common ground.

On the other hand, it's also important to leave room for objections. If someone objects, they are doing so because they want to protect the circle from undermining its own progress - for example, if we stretch ourselves too thin by starting an additional project, we can't do good quality work in our regular activities - the objection helps us notice that.

In that sense, objections are a gift because they help us make avoidable mistakes.

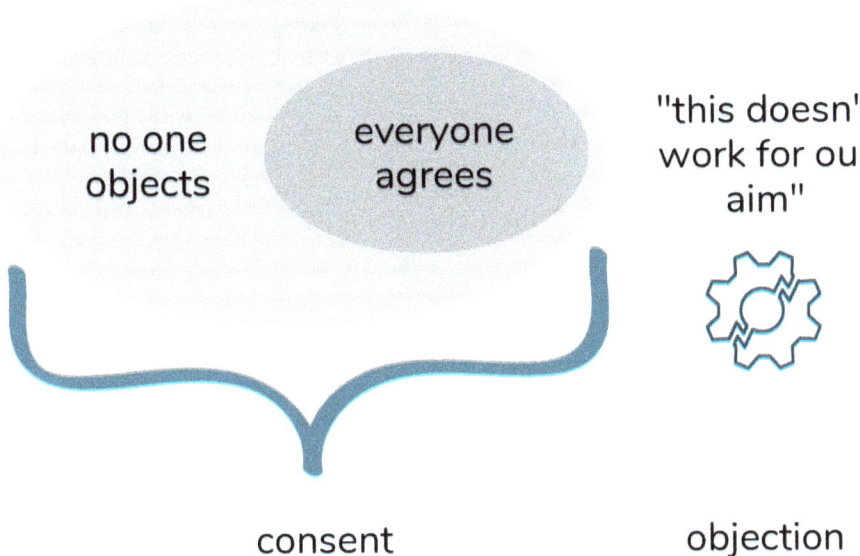

If someone doesn't have an objection, that means they consent.
If someone doesn't consent, they are asked to share their objection.

The circle tries to integrate the objection together.

If there is an objection, try to understand it. Remember that the member is likely to see something that everyone missed so tune in and try to see what they are seeing.

If someone objects...

Understand the objection

Do a round to find solutions.

Make a new proposal and ask for consent again.

To you really understand? Reflect back what you hear and check.

If someone objects, facilitators don't have to "fix" it alone. Tap into the group's ideas.

Facilitators pick suggestions and combine them into a new proposal.

ideas!

Options for integrating objections

Most groups jump to modifications to integrate an objection - but try other method as well! Sometimes we don't even need to change the proposal, we just need to set an evaluation date or agree to pay attention to a metric or a potential negative impact.

Modify the proposal!

What part of the proposal can you change so it works?

Shorten the term

Shorten the term - are people willing to try it out for a shorter time period?

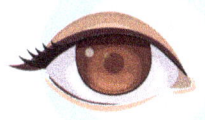

Measure the concern

Commit to paying attention. Could you move forward while tracking the impact of the proposal?

Selection process

If there are given choices and you need to pick one, use the selection process.
The selecting process is most often used for selecting people for roles.

It can also be use to select a venue, theme, amount or name.

Understanding the role

- Clarifying questions on role description
- Qualifications for role?
- Consent on list of qualifications

Is the role description clear?

In a round, gather qualifications you'd like to see in the person holding the role.

Approve the list.

Explore options

- Write down nominations
- Nomination round (say why)
- Change round

Ask everyone to write down who they nominate for the role(s). People can nominate themselves!

In a round, let everyone share their nomination along with reasons for their nominate.

In a second round, people can change their nomination based on other people's nominations.

Decide

- Propose candidate
- Decide by consent
- Celebrate and publish

The facilitator proposes a candidate and a term.

Do a consent round - integrate objections as needed.

Don't forget to celebrate!

Filling roles is like wearing a hat for a while.

(The image doesn't quite carry over because one often has more than one role but it's unusual to wear more than one hat.)

Defining roles in role descriptions

To define a role within a meeting, do rounds on aim & activities and then on constraints for the role. Add rounds on hours/week and/or pay if needed.

Then synthesize the information and ask for consent on the role.

It's like defining a special hat - later you can decide who will wear it.

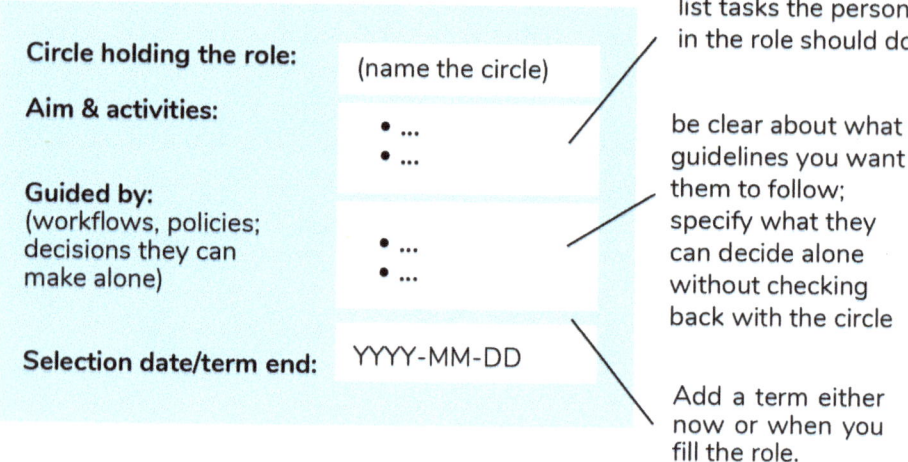

list tasks the person in the role should do

be clear about what guidelines you want them to follow; specify what they can decide alone without checking back with the circle

Add a term either now or when you fill the role.

Then fill the role (proposal + consent or by using the selection process p. 19)

Drafting a proposal

There are different ways to draft a proposal, depending on time and complexity of the issue:

- Have one person write it.
- Doing rounds for input and synthesizing it on the spot.
- Doing rounds and asking someone to synthesize it between meetings.
- Ask around for a template

Drafting a proposal - full process

Picture forming and proposal shaping on our cleaning policy

Dimensions	Proposal ideas	Proposal
Who cleans? How often? Cleaning supplies Trash Surfaces Deep cleaning? What if it's NOT clean?	Everyone cleans once a month. Rotating system Cleaning supplies provided, maintained by office manager. Cleaner on duty also does surfaces and trash & recycling Pay for deep cleaning every 6 months If you don't clean, you get a second chance, then you have to clean 2 shifts.	Now synthesize into a proposal

For complex proposals, we recommend this process, called **picture forming and proposal shaping.**
1. Make a list of considerations (some people call them 'dimensions')
2. Gather ideas on each consideration It's ok if the proposal ideas overlap or contradict, just write them down.
3. Synthesize the proposal ideas into one proposal.

Facilitating a performance review
- A group giving feedback to one person

A performance review helps the alignment in a group by creating an opportunity for a circle (or several people from different circles) to see the world from one person's — the focus person's — point of view and offering their feedback.

We zoom in on that focus person's roles successes and learnings and give them impulses for changes that would improve the collaboration.

It's important to note that in all rounds, the focus person speaks first - that way, the process happens **with** them and not **to** them.

The process might sound long and dreadful but it's deeply satisfying and connecting to have a place to say the unsaid things - both for the focus person and the members of the performance review circle.

The circle can be a regular circle or an group assembled of different circles to provide a 360 degree view of a person's roles in different circles.

Performance review

Understanding performance

Clarifying roles, previous improvement plans — What role(s) is the person filling? What's the current expectation??

What went well? — Round of appreciations

What could have been improved? — Round of things that need improvement

Explore improvements

Dimensions: improvement areas — Identify dimensions to focus on

Improvement ideas — Concrete ideas on how to work on the dimensions. What could the point person do?

Synthesize ideas — Compile into an improvement plan

Decide

Consent process for the improvement plan

Facilitating a circle review
- Everyone in a group giving feedback to everyone

Focus person 1

Focus person reflects about their own contribution and performance in the circle.

The circle reflects on their performance in a reaction round.

The focus person responds to the reactions with their reflection.

Focus person 2, 3, 4, 5...

same process with a new focus person

Be aware!
This process takes a long time in groups bigger than 6 people.

This process is unifying and connecting by providing shared reality.
It is great for surfacing interdependencies and differences in perception.

Most times, people are worried because they are very self-critical, and then relieved and touched when they realize how much coworkers do see and appreciate them.

Try it out!

All the pieces fit together

Please keep in mind that meeting facilitation not only depends on the facilitator. A lot of pieces need to fit together for an organization to run well.

Here are just a few examples:

Structure and clarity
- Are roles and circle aims defined well?
- Are group sizes manageable (best group size is under 8)
- Are roles and accountabilities defined well so work happens outside of meetings?

Interpersonal
- Is there trust?
- Are people willing and able to give honest feedback?
- Are people personally aligned with the aim?

Learning and skills
- Do people have the experience and skills to follow a meeting and contribute?

Common questions

Consent

What if someone brings a reaction during questions? Or a reaction during the consent round?

Be generous. Thank for them their contribution, ask them to remember it so it can be heard later. Then ask them whether they have questions (or whatever the prompt of the round is.)

How can we make a consent decision if circle members are absent?

Technically, you can't. There are several workarounds, and it's good as a circle to decide on an absentee policy so you know what to do in those moments.
- Option A: have every circle member consent and ask for consent from absent circle members later. (The decision is only made after everyone consents.)
- Option B: make a policy that people who are absent can't object. (Carries the risk of power struggles and deterioration of trust)
- Option C: ask circle members' opinions on proposals before the meeting. (Leaves lack of clarity if the proposed changes with amendments during the meeting.)

What if someone wants to abstain in a consent round?

In a consent round, no circle member can abstain or "stand aside". We need to hear from every circle member to determine whether there is consent for the proposal and to integrate objections.
- Maybe they don't really care about the proposal? That means they don't object = they consent.
- If they don't like the proposal and, for example, don't want to be 'responsible' for it, ask them for their concerns and treat them as objections. Hearing their input will be valuable no matter what you label them as.

Can amendments be added to the proposal after the quick reaction round? (Or just after the consent round?)

The safest moment to amend is after an objection.

But sometimes, reactions to a proposal surface good improvements that can be used to modify the proposal instantly. The only caveat is that groups are encouraged not to spend too much time perfecting the proposal (since that's most likely not time-efficient), and that tweaking the proposal too much can water it down or make it incoherent.
Often, groups start rushing at the end and might add amendments without thinking them through in the context of the whole proposal. Therefore be extra cautious when amending the proposal "on the fly".
Also, be sure that every circle member is aware of the modifications before consenting.

Objections: What is the difference between a "negative reaction" and an "objection"?

A negative reaction can be pointing to an objection or just to a preference. On the other hand, one can object to a proposal without experiencing a negative reaction. So there really is only a loose connection between both terms.

Having an objection means to see harm in the proposal with regard to the aim of the circle, so it's more about whether the proposal **works**, not whether one (dis)likes it.

Meetings

 **Who is responsible for timekeeping?**

Everyone. The circle approves their agenda by consenting to it, ideally including time information for each agenda item. Everyone is responsible for keeping the meeting close to that agenda. If this is impossible, the agenda needs to be adjusted with everyone's consent.
By selecting a facilitator (by consent), the circle gives some authority to the facilitator for making operational decisions to allow the circle to stay in their agreed-upon time frame. For example, the facilitator might choose to time each member's contribution in a round, or might choose to move to consent without a second reaction round, etc.
The facilitator is generally asked to "police" the circle transparently, kindly and with consideration. The circle is asked to be considerate and intentional in how they follow the approved agenda.

 **What are your thoughts on rotating facilitation?**

In general, this is possible and can be desired to give more people a chance to get experience. The potential downside is that if the role of the facilitator includes preparing the meeting, this often doesn't happen with rotating facilitation.
Find a way to make sure meetings are just as well prepared by rotating facilitators as they would be with ongoing facilitators. Also, with rotating facilitation, it can be hard to improve because facilitation situations are too infrequent.
A better strategy to give more people more experience is to make short terms, for example, every 4 meetings.

How do we manage emotional safety in groups where members have a history together?

Address it. This could mean that the individuals or groups do some restorative work as a group or outside of the group. It is typically not sustainable to sweet these dynamics under the carpet.

Why only one round of reactions during decisions? What if we need more time?

The quick reaction round comes after clarifying questions in the consent decision-making pattern and responds to the question "What do I think about this proposal?" This is a round where almost anything goes. We can say what we want about the proposal. Whatever is alive within at that moment. We might voice concerns, confusion, opportunities, what we like, what we don't like, or we might not say anything at all.

A perfectly legitimate quick reaction is that you need more time to consider the proposal. A main part of the intent of quick reactions is to identify which parts of a proposal are generating easy approval and which parts are triggering confusion or concerns, so that we can focus attention on those elements of a proposal that need more time.

Other

How does one accept a new member into a circle? Is there a process for that?

Yes! It's a simple consent process of the proposal that XYZ join the circle.
Welcome the person, ask them questions about their why or their skills, do a round of reactions and then consent.
One can only object to a new person on the basis of there being harm.

Can one lose circle membership?

A circle member can be removed from a circle.
Circle membership is a decision that requires consent. If someone's circle membership is not within the range of tolerance of some other circle members anymore, we can propose to remove that person. That person will not have the right to object.
This will only be done if that person's circle membership keeps the circle from achieving its aim, for example, because the emotional disturbance is distracting and seems avoidable.
Note that removing someone from a circle is not necessarily the same as removing someone from the organization. Depending on the nature of the organization and its membership model, that person might remain a member, or might remain or become a member of a different circle where those issues might not arise.

What do we do if someone is upset or sad in a meeting?

Assuming the behavior is disruptive to the meeting and depending on the circumstances, you could
(a) do a reaction round
(b) invite the member to speak about what is going on for them and then ask them what they request from the circle followed up with a reaction round of reflective listening or empathy before hearing the focus member speak again.
(c) Ask another circle member to support them outside of the meeting while the meeting continues or after it ends.
(d) Take a 5-minute break or a minute of silence
(e) any combination of these options.

How is conflict in circles handled?

Listenings, mediation, restorative circles. These are not specific to Sociocracy.

For simple conflicts, put them on the agenda and do rounds, i.e., how do we understand our conflict, what is something that is safe enough to try so we get some feedback and keep learning and moving with experience. Rather than stay stuck in righteousness or fear.

Ultimately if a circle cannot make a decision the issue is passed on to the higher circle for decision.

Every organization should also have a conflict resolution process and support from a role so conflict can be addressed.

Books (full books)

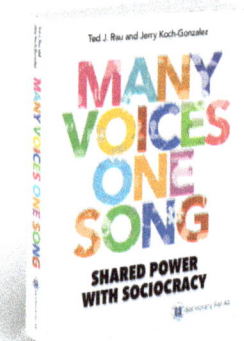

The manual about sociocracy. Packed with information, examples, diagrams and an index. Find deeper explanations about all the processes and situations.

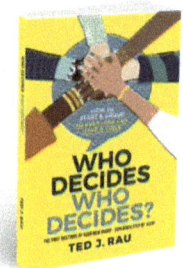

A simple step-by-step guide for starting a group sociocratically. Best for groups 2-12 people.

Educators and parents! Use sociocracy with children to teach responsible and caring decision-making.

Small booklets in this series

A general overview of sociocracy (70 pages)

A booklet for role holders (70 pages)

>> www.sociocracyforall.org/books

Meeting format

Opening Round

ADMIN
1. Attendance
2. Duration
3. Minutes
4. Information
5. Next meeting

Consent to agenda

Agenda Items

Report
Share and understand information

Exploration
Listen to reactions and ideas

Decision
Make a decision

Update Backlog

Closing Round

with feedback on
- process
- content
- interpersonal

 Sociocracy For All

Download this template on our website

Checklists

Formed a new circle?
- [ ] Aim(s)
- [ ] Domain
- [ ] Term for evaluation
- [ ] Membership
- [ ] Conveners/links

Complete proposal
- [ ] Final wording
- [ ] Term for evaluation
- [ ] Metrics for evaluation
- [ ] Feedback plan
- [ ] Publication and implementation

Defined a new role?
- [ ] Activities/tasks/aims
- [ ] Define authority
- [ ] Term

Co-create a proposal

Understand
- What is the context? The underlying needs? Synthesise into a needs statement.

Explore
- Picture forming: dimensions?
- Proposal shaping: proposal ideas?

Decide
- Synthesize into a proposal
- Decide by consent

Selection process

Understand role
- Clarifying questions on role description
- Qualifications for role?
- Consent on list of qualifications

Explore options
- Write down nominations
- Nomination round (say why)
- Change round

Decide
- Propose candidate
- Decide by consent
- Celebrate and publish

Decide by consent

Understand
- Present a proposal
- Clarifying questions round

Explore
- Quick reactions round

Decide
- Re-state the proposal (with amendments, if any)
- Consent or objections round
- Integrate any objections
- Celebrate and publish

(Make sure every decision has a review term.)

Integrate objections

Understand the objection(s)
- Clarifying questions round

Explore options
- Modify the proposal (to address the concern)
- Shorten the term
- Measure the concern (to track the concern)

Decide
- Synthesize amendments
- State the amended proposal
- Decide by consent

Circle minutes coverpage template

ABOUT THIS CIRCLE

Aim(s)		Review Term	
Domain		2022-11-22	
Circle Members	Name (email address); name (email address)		
Parent Circle	Circle name & link to circle's document		
Sub-Circles	• Circle name & link to circle's document		
Circle email address			
Circle Folder			
Objectives & Key Results			
Key Links			

ROLES

Process Roles	Name & email address	Review Term
Leader — supports circle operations		2022-11-22
Delegate — second voice in parent circle		2022-11-22
Facilitator — facilitates meetings		2022-11-22
Secretary — minute-taking and docs admin		2022-11-22

Operational Roles	Name & email address	Review Term
		2022-11-22
		2022-11-22
		2022-11-22

OTHER POLICIES

Policy Title	Brief Description	Term
		2022-11-22
		2022-11-22
		2022-11-22
		2022-11-22

Download this template on our website

BACKLOG

Due date	Priority	Description	Desired Outcome	Holder
2022-11-22	!!!		Exploration	
2022-11-22	!!		Report	
2022-11-22	!		Report	
2022-11-22	²		Report	

You can sort this table by due date by Format > Table > sort ascending

Circle minutes meeting template

MEETING AGENDA TEMPLATE

2023-01-01 at 00:00 UTC

TIME & DURATION		MEETING'S LOCATION/LINK:	OUTCOME
00:00	10	**OPENING ROUND / CHECK-IN** (no notes)	
00:10	5	**ADMIN**	
		Attendance – *who's here and filling roles?*	
		→ **Facilitator**: name | **Secretary**: name | **Leader**: name | **Delegate**: name | **Other members**: names | **Guests**: names	
		Duration – *does anyone need to leave earlier?*	
		→ 1h30m	
		Minutes – *anything needing attention from the previous meeting's minutes?*	
		→	
		Information – *any announcements?*	
		→	
		Next meeting – *when and where?*	
		→ 2023-01-01 at 00:00 for 00 minutes	
00:15	2	**CONSENT TO AGENDA**	Decision
00:17	3	**ACTION ITEMS ACCOUNTABILITY** – *noted from previous meeting* ☐ ☐ ☐	Report
00:20	10	**REPORTS** Parent Circle Report – Leader: name • Sub-Circles Report – Delegate: name • Op Roles & Projects Reports – Role/Project Holder: name •	Report
00:30	15	**AGENDA ITEM**	Exploration
00:45	15	**AGENDA ITEM**	Report
1:00	10	**AGENDA ITEM**	Report
1:10	5	**ACTION ITEMS RECAP** – *to paste under next meeting's Action Items Accountability* ☐	Report
1:15	5	**BACKLOG UPDATE**	Exploration
1:20	10	**CLOSING ROUND / CHECK-OUT** – *feedback on content, interpersonal, processes*	

Download this template on our website

Role description template

[Role name]

Circle holding the role:

Aim & activities

Guided by:
(workflows, policies; decisions they can make alone, etc.)

Qualifications

Handoffs to other circles/roles

More context?

Hours/week or month

Pay

Important links etc.

Role review date
(Review of the role itself)

Current *holder* of the role: **Term:**

Leader of the circle (current)

Selection date:

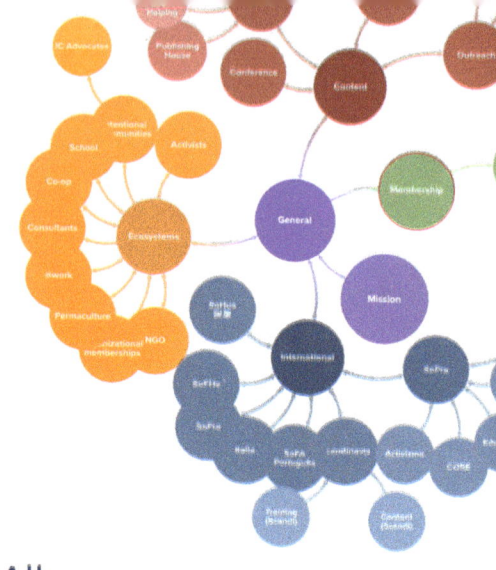

Sociocracy For All is a member-run nonprofit that offers training and consulting for individuals and groups at all levels.

Topics:
- Decision-making by consent
- Organizational structure
- Inclusive meetings
- Performance and accountability

- Facilitation practice
- Immersion programs
- Conflict resolution
- Nonviolent Communication for meeting facilitation
- Certification programs

See our training offerings: www.sociocracyforall.org/training

www.ingramcontent.com/pod-product-compliance
Lightning Source LLC
Chambersburg PA
CBHW061804070526
44586CB00023B/2711